Skiing

in Action

John Crossingham & Bobbie Kalman

Crabtree Publishing Company

www.crabtreebooks.com

Created by Bobbie Kalman

Dedicated by Margaret Amy Reiach
To Sarah and Megan—see you on the slopes!

Editor-in-Chief
Bobbie Kalman

Writing team
John Crossingham
Bobbie Kalman

Substantive editor
Kelley MacAulay

Project editor
Kristina Lundblad

Editors
Molly Aloian
Amanda Bishop
Kathryn Smithyman

Art Director
Robert MacGregor

Design
Margaret Amy Reiach

Production Coordinator
Katherine Kantor

Photo research
Crystal Foxton

Consultant
Paul Robbins, Senior Correspondent, United States Ski
and Snowboard Association

Special thanks to
Natasha Barrett, Jacqueline Everson, Emma Funnel, Ethan
Funnel, Nicholas Cassara, Olivia Leslie, Chris Jones, Jamie
Bull, Lesley Jannis, and Horseshoe Resort

Photographs
Marc Crabtree: back cover, pages 7, 8, 9, 14, 15, 17, 18, 19, 20,
    21, 23, 25 (bottom)
Mark Ashkanasy/STL/Icon SMI: pages 27, 30 (top)
Paul Martinez/PHOTOSPORT.COM: page 31 (bottom)
Philippe Millereau/ DPPI/Icon SMI: page 26 (bottom)
STL/Icon SMI: page 26 (top)
Shazamm: page 29 (top)
Other images by Adobe Image Library, Corbis Images, Corel,
Digital Stock, and PhotoDisc

Illustrations
All illustrations by Bonna Rouse

Crabtree Publishing Company

www.crabtreebooks.com   1-800-387-7650

Cataloging-in-Publication Data
Crossingham, John.
    Skiing in action / John Crossingham & Bobbie Kalman.
        p. cm. -- (Sports in action)
    Includes index.
    ISBN 0-7787-0337-1 (RLB) -- ISBN 0-7787-0357-6 (pbk.)
    1. Skis and skiing--Juvenile literature. [1. Skis and skiing.]
I. Kalman, Bobbie. II. Title. III. Series.
    GV854.315.C76 2004
    796.93--dc22
                                                        2004011119
                                                        LC

**Published in
the United States**

PMB16A
350 Fifth Ave.
Suite 3308
New York, NY
10118

**Published
in Canada**

616 Welland Ave.,
St. Catharines, Ontario,
Canada
L2M 5V6

**Published in the
United Kingdom**

73 Lime Walk
Headington
Oxford
OX3 7AD
United Kingdom

**Published
in Australia**

386 Mt. Alexander Rd.,
Ascot Vale (Melbourne)
VIC 3032

Contents

What is skiing?

Skiing is a winter sport that involves people sliding over snow on **skis**. Skis are long, thin runners made of **fiberglass**. Skiers wear boots that attach to the skis. There are several types of skiing. Two types that are popular today are **nordic** and **alpine**. Nordic skiing includes **cross-country**, **ski jumping**, and **biathlon**. Alpine skiing is often called "downhill" skiing. Alpine skiers ride down large, snow-covered mountains. This book teaches the basics of alpine skiing.

Recreational or competitive?

Most skiers, including beginners, enjoy **recreational** skiing, which is skiing just for fun. Some advanced skiers enter **competitions**, such as alpine racing. In alpine racing, skiers perform tight turns as they speed down steep **slopes**, or hillsides. The racer with the fastest time wins.

*Two other skiing styles include **freeskiing** and **freestyle**. Freeskiers search mountainsides to find new slopes and ski over untouched snow. Freestyle skiers perform daring **tricks**, or moves, in midair or as they ski down the slopes.*

A long history

Skiing has been a form of transportation for thousands of years. Scandinavian people used simple wooden skis to travel from place to place over snow in winter. Today, skiing is both a competitive sport and a form of recreation.

The essentials

A skier's most important equipment is a good pair of skis. Skis come in many styles. The styles are designed to match the abilities of different skiers. Your height, weight, and skill level will affect the width, length, flexibility, and **cut** of your skis. When buying or renting equipment, make sure you talk with the store clerk about your height, weight, and skiing style.

basket

grip

The poles

Ski poles provide skiers with **stability** and extra pushing power. Each pole has a **grip** at the top that a skier holds. A **basket** at the end of the pole stops the pole from sinking too deeply into the snow.

The skis

For decades, downhill skis had straight **edges**, or sides. In the early 1990s, however, **shaped skis** were introduced. Shaped skis have **sidecuts**, or sides that curve inward. The design of shaped skis makes them faster and easier to turn. Shaped skis are very popular because they are easier to use than straight skis are.

The boots

Ski boots have tough plastic **shells**, or outer coverings. They also have **inner boots**, which are thick padded liners that cushion the feet and help keep them warm. **Bindings** lock around the toe and heel of the boot and are used to attach the boots to the skis. To get your boot into a binding, point your toe down and slip it into the front binding. Then push your heel down hard into the rear binding. The binding snaps in place and grips your boot. Most bindings are released by pulling up on the rear binding. The bindings will also automatically release your boots if you take a tumble down a ski hill.

Bundle up!

Skiing is usually done in very cold weather, so proper clothing is important. Most skiers wear layers of clothing. Layers keep you warm when the weather is cold, but they can also be removed if the day warms up. The first layer consists of long, **thermal underwear** and thick socks. These clothes stay close to the skin and lock in heat. The next layer may include pants, a turtleneck, and a warm pullover. A jacket and snow pants make up the outer layer. The outer layer of clothing should be windproof and waterproof. Nothing can ruin a day of skiing like wet clothes can! Finally, you'll need a winter hat and gloves or mittens.

Extra protection

Cold weather can **chap**, or dry and crack, the skin. You can use lip balm to protect your lips against the cold and wind. You also need to use sunblock on your face. It is very easy to get a sunburn while skiing because snow reflects the sun back onto your face. A pair of **goggles** keeps the wind and snow out of your eyes so that you can see clearly. You should also bring along a little snack, such as some fruit or a small granola bar. You can carry these items in your pockets.

Lodges and lifts

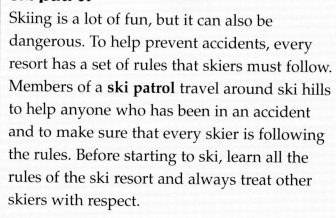

*The easiest and shortest slopes at a resort are sometimes called **bunny hills**. Bunny hills are perfect hills for beginners.*

Most skiers visit ski resorts to hit the slopes. Every ski resort has a main **lodge**, which is a large building usually found at the base of a hill. The lodge provides skiers with everything they need for a fun day of skiing, including restrooms, cafeterias, equipment rentals, lessons, and first-aid services. Ski resorts with more than one hill may have more than one lodge.

Ticket to ride

The main lodge is usually where you buy your **lift ticket**. The lift ticket allows you to ride the **lifts**, or machines that carry you up the ski hills. The lift ticket is a sticker or tag that attaches to your jacket. Make sure you don't lose it, or you'll be stuck at the bottom of the hill!

Ski patrol

Skiing is a lot of fun, but it can also be dangerous. To help prevent accidents, every resort has a set of rules that skiers must follow. Members of a **ski patrol** travel around ski hills to help anyone who has been in an accident and to make sure that every skier is following the rules. Before starting to ski, learn all the rules of the ski resort and always treat other skiers with respect.

Catching a lift

The most common type of lift is the **chair lift**. A chair lift has a **safety bar**, or a bar that holds skiers in their seats. Some chairs also have **foot rests**. You can place your skis on a foot rest during the ride. Chair lifts are named for the number of people they carry—**singles** (one person), **doubles** (two people), **triples** (three people), or **quads** (four people). Triples and quads are common because they can move many people at once. There are also six-seater chair lifts.

Other lifts

Surface lifts and **gondolas** are two other types of lifts. Surface lifts include **rope tows** and **T-bars**. On these lifts, your skis stay on the snow and you are pulled up the hill as you hold on to a rope or bar. These lifts are less common than chair lifts are, but you can still find them at smaller resorts or on bunny hills. A gondola is a fully enclosed compartment that carries up to twelve people up a hill. Gondolas are found at very large resorts that have many skiers.

All aboard!

Getting on a chair lift is easy! When it is your turn to board, place both your poles in one hand. Look over your outside shoulder and reach out with your empty hand to guide yourself into the seat. The chair will move in behind your knees, so you can simply sit down. When everyone on the chair is settled, lower the safety bar. If there is a foot rest, place your skis on it. To get off the chair lift, raise the safety bar just before you reach the ramp. Use your hands to shove yourself off the seat and then ski down the ramp.

*If you are nervous about getting on a chair lift, ask the **lift attendant** to slow it down.*

Trails and snow

Paths used for skiing are called **runs** or **trails**. A typical ski resort will have 30 to over 100 different runs. Before hitting the slopes, it's best to know what kind of snow you'll be skiing on. Ideal snow is soft and smooth but firm and easy to grip, even after hundreds of skiers have passed over it. Slushy snow is wet and thick, making the bottom of your skis stick to it. **Powder** is deep, soft snow. It is popular with advanced skiers.

Skiers need to build up great speed to ski through powder without sinking into the snow. Ice is almost impossible for skis to grip. It is best to avoid skiing on ice—you can usually spot ice because it is shinier than the snow around it. If there is not enough snow covering the trails, resorts often use snowblowers to create **machine-made snow**. Machine-made snow is harder and icier than natural snow is.

*Ski trails are often **groomed**, or smoothed out, by large vehicles that flatten and spread the snow across the trail to provide an even surface. The small ridges created by the grooming vehicles are sometimes called **corduroy**.*

Learning the signs

Trails are ranked according to their difficulty so that skiers of all skill levels can find the perfect slopes. The slopes are graded using a simple series of colors and shapes, shown right. The grades for each slope will appear on your trail map. Below is an example of how a trail map looks.

 Green circle runs *have gentle slopes and smooth surfaces. They are perfect for beginners.*

 Blue square runs *are similar to green runs, but with slightly steeper slopes, rougher bumps, and quicker turns.*

 Black diamond runs *are very difficult. They are steep and often narrow. They usually include a series of bumps called* **moguls***.*

 Double-black diamond runs *are extremely difficult! They are for experts only.*

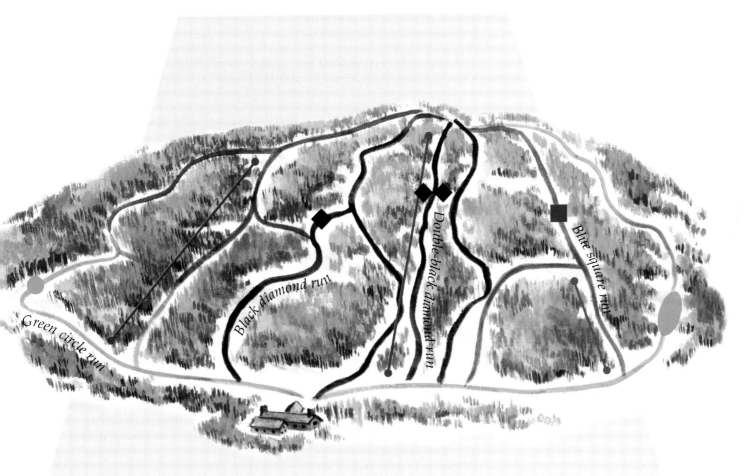

Green circle run

Black diamond run

Double-black diamond run

Blue square run

Most resorts use red or black lines to show where the lifts run. **Terrain parks** *and* **halfpipes***, where freestyle skiers and snowboarders can perform tricks, are usually marked with an orange oval.*

Warming up

Skiing is a sport that requires you to use your entire body. Trails are sometimes bumpy, so falls can be expected, especially for beginners. Skiing with cold, stiff muscles can easily lead to cramps and minor injuries. To warm up your body, walk around briskly for five or ten minutes and then perform the warm-ups and stretches shown on these pages. Some of these stretches cannot be done in ski boots, so do them in the lodge just before going outside to put on your skis.

Leg crossovers
While standing, cross your legs at the ankles. Bend at the waist and slowly reach for your toes. Keep your knees slightly bent and stretch as far as you can without becoming uncomfortable. Hold the stretch for ten seconds and then straighten up and switch legs. Stretch each leg three times.

Quadriceps stretch
Stand on your right foot and lift up your left leg behind you. Grab your ankle with your left hand. Keep your knees close together. You will feel a stretch in the muscles in the front of your left leg. Hold the stretch for a count of ten and then switch legs.

Trunk circles

Put your hands on your hips and place your feet shoulder-width apart. Keep your feet flat on the floor as you swing your hips around in circles. Do three circles to the right and three to the left.

Lunges

Stand with your feet shoulder-width apart. Take a big step forward with your left leg. When your foot touches down, position your left knee directly over your ankle. Bend your right knee so that your heel lifts off the ground. With your left leg, push yourself back to the starting position. Repeat the lunge movement with your right leg. Do ten lunges with each leg.

Ankle rotations

Sit with one leg extended straight in front of you. Bend your other leg so that you can grab your foot. Gently move your foot in circles. When you have done ten circles, do ten more in the other direction. Remember to change legs!

"V" stretch

Sit with your legs in a "V" and flex your feet so your toes are pointing up. Keeping your lower back straight, lean forward until you feel a stretch in the back of your legs and buttocks. Hold the stretch for a count of ten.

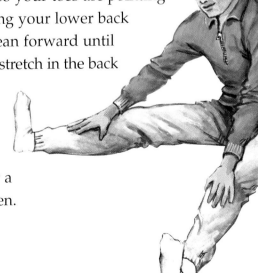

Keep your balance!

Skiing is all about balance. Equipment that fits properly provides you with stability, but you must also hold your body in a balanced **stance**. A stance is made up of the position of your feet, legs, and upper body as you ski. In a basic skiing stance, shown left, your knees are slightly bent and your skis are close together but not touching. Your poles are ready to be **planted**, or firmly placed, at any time, and your head is up. Keep your arms slightly forward to help you balance.

Get a feel for it

Standing on skis for the first time can feel strange. Before you go up a hill, take some time to get comfortable. Simple exercises such as walking forward on your skis can help. Concentrate on keeping your skis **parallel**, or right alongside each other, and about six inches (15.2 cm) apart. With each step, plant the opposite pole for extra balance. For example, when you step with your right ski, plant your left pole.

Pole position

Your poles also provide extra stability—especially while turning. Plant the pole in the snow as you turn. Grip it using your thumb and your first finger. Keep the other three fingers loose so the pole can swing back and forth.

14

Good advice

A great ski instructor is essential when you are first learning to ski. Ski lessons are the best way to improve your skills and prevent you from developing bad habits. Even good skiers sometimes take advanced classes to polish their skills and learn new tricks. Most resorts offer lessons for skiers of all skill levels. When you sign up for a lesson, be honest about your abilities and what you want to learn. Taking a class that is too advanced will leave you behind, but signing up for a class that is too easy will bore you!

On edge

The words **"uphill"** and **"downhill"** are used a lot in skiing. Uphill and downhill are directions—up the hill and down the hill. Skiers also use the words "uphill" and "downhill" to describe their skis. Your **uphill ski** is the one that is closer to the top of the hill when you are standing sideways. Your **downhill ski** is the one that is closer to the bottom of the hill.

uphill ski

downhill ski

Out or in?

The edges of a ski are known by several names, depending on how they are being used. The **inside edge** is the side of the ski that is closest to your other ski when you are wearing both skis. The **outside edge** is on the opposite side.

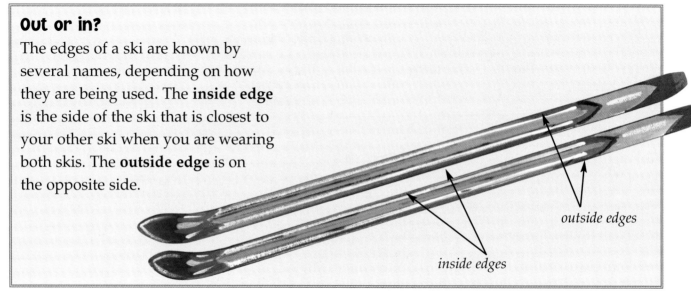

outside edges

inside edges

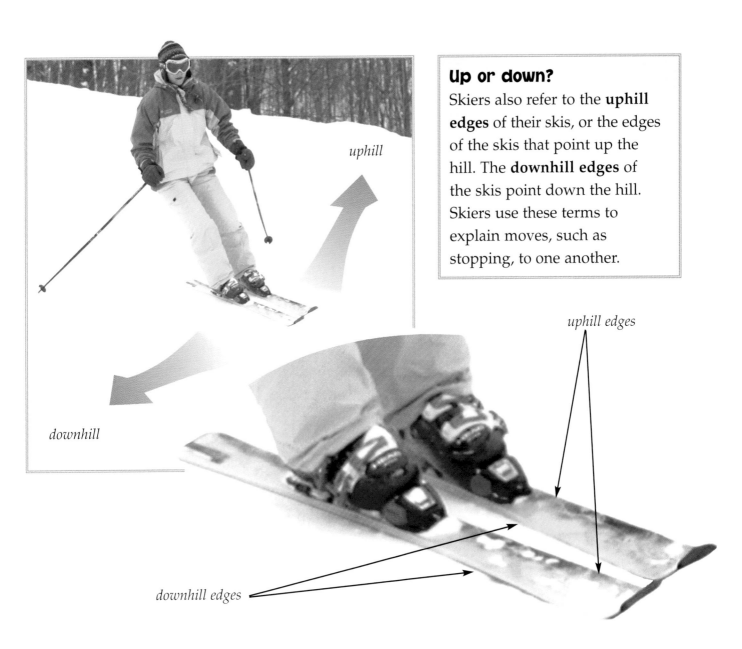

uphill

downhill

Up or down?
Skiers also refer to the **uphill edges** of their skis, or the edges of the skis that point up the hill. The **downhill edges** of the skis point down the hill. Skiers use these terms to explain moves, such as stopping, to one another.

uphill edges

downhill edges

Getting an edge

Once you know which edge is which, learning to use your edges will be easy. When you press down on either edge of your ski, it digs in and grips the snow. This grip gives you control over your direction and speed. Get a feel for your edges before you hit the slopes.

Stand in one spot and roll one of your ankles outward, so that your outside edge grips the snow. Balance on that edge. Then roll your ankle to the other side to use the other edge. Hold each position as long as you can without falling over.

Before starting out...

When you're visiting a ski resort, you won't always be skiing down the hill. It's important to know a few basic moves so that you can get from place to place, even when you aren't racing down the mountainside. **Skating** is a move that allows you to glide quickly over flat **terrain** or uphill for short distances. The **side-step** allows you to move short distances up or down a hill. You use the edges of your skis while skating and side-stepping.

The great skate
The quickest way to travel over flat snow is to skate. Skating is done by gliding over the snow. While skating, each ski first glides and then pushes.

1. Point the tip of your right ski outward. Dig the inside edge of your right ski into the snow. Push off with your right ski and glide forward on your left ski.

2. As you glide, bring your right ski back on the ground next to your left. Now repeat the push, using your left ski. Glide forward on your right ski.

Side-stepping

Sometimes you'll find yourself a little too far down or up the hill from where you wanted to stop. You can use the side-step to move slightly uphill or downhill.

1. To climb, lean on your uphill edges with your skis pointing across the slope. Lift up the leg that is closer to the top of the hill.

2. Take a big step to the side.

3. Now lift your other leg up. Use your poles for balance.

4. Place your leg down beside the uphill leg.

A bone to pick

A more advanced way to climb is to do the **herringbone climb**. In this climb, your skis form a "V" with the tips pointing outward, and you face up the hill. You must use your inside edges to grip the snow as you step up the slope.

Both the side-step and herringbone climb are tiring. Use them only for climbing short distances.

19

Ready to go!

shallow traverse

steep traverse

fall line

If you rolled a ball down a slope, it would follow an imaginary line called a **fall line**. The fall line is the fastest, most direct way down the slope, but this path is much too fast for most skiers to take! Before heading down a slope, you need to learn how to **traverse**, or move across the slope. Traversing allows you to control your speed. The closer skiers come to following the fall line, the faster they go. Skiing close to the fall line is known as a **steep traverse**. Beginners use a **shallow traverse**, which is much wider than the fall line.

Skiing a traverse

Start a shallow traverse with your skis pointed across the slope. To gain some speed, push off with your poles or lean slightly forward by pressing your shins against the front of your boots. When traversing, you must press down on your uphill edges. Your stance is much like the basic stance on page 14, but your upper body is pointed slightly downhill. Your uphill ski should also be slightly ahead of your other ski. This stance not only helps you move forward, but it also puts you in a good position to turn.

Stop this thing!

Once you learn how to traverse, you need to know how to stop! Many beginners stop by using a move called the **snowplow**—they point their ski tips together to form an upside-down "V" and dig in their inside edges. As you become more comfortable on your skis, you may prefer to **skid** to a stop. To skid, quickly and firmly push down with your heels and dig your uphill edges hard into the snow. Bend your knees and lean slightly uphill to keep your balance. Hold your arms forward. The harder you push into the snow, the faster you will come to a stop.

As you skid, your body will turn until you are sliding down the hill sideways.

Getting back up

All skiers fall down sometimes, but there are ways to soften the tumble. Falling downhill can lead to injuries. If you know you are about to fall, try falling backward into the slope. Falling backward helps you stay in the same place on the slope. If you have fallen, you can use your poles to lift yourself back up. Place the poles together and plant them just uphill of your knees. Wrap your uphill hand around the middle of the poles and place your other hand around the grips. Lift yourself up by pushing down on your poles.

After a fall, use your poles to help you get back up. Don't stay down for too long—oncoming skiers may not be able to see you.

Changing direction

Almost all your time on the slope is
spent traversing and then turning. Turns
not only let you change direction, but they
also help you control your speed. Turning is
often the skill that beginners find most difficult to learn,
but by taking things slowly and concentrating, your turns
will soon be smooth and controlled. The first simple rule
of turning is not to turn with your upper body. Most of
the turning movement takes place below your waist.

Carving turns

Smooth, wide turns are called **carving turns** because they carve through the snow, leaving perfect trails behind. Practice carving turns on a wide run with a gentle slope.

1. Begin a turn by traversing on your uphill edges. Slide your uphill ski ahead of your other ski. Bend your knees and press down on the downhill edges of your skis. You will start to turn toward the fall line.

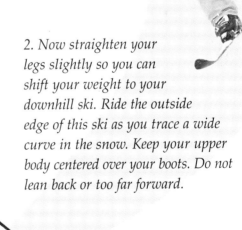

2. Now straighten your legs slightly so you can shift your weight to your downhill ski. Ride the outside edge of this ski as you trace a wide curve in the snow. Keep your upper body centered over your boots. Do not lean back or too far forward.

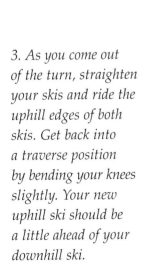

3. As you come out of the turn, straighten your skis and ride the uphill edges of both skis. Get back into a traverse position by bending your knees slightly. Your new uphill ski should be a little ahead of your downhill ski.

Built for speed

While making short-radius turns, your chest points downhill at all times.

A few smooth carved turns are all you need on gentle slopes. As hills get steeper, however, you need to traverse less and turn more to stay in control. Turns done one right after the other without any traversing are called **short-radius turns**. While doing these turns, you constantly shift your weight from one ski to the other. Work up to making short-radius turns. Every time you ski, attempt slightly steeper hills and work on making shorter traverses between turns.

S-s-super turns

After you have made a few short-radius turns, stop and look back at your path. Do you see smooth S-shaped curves or jagged lines? Although you made quick turns, your path should show that your turns flowed into one another as you carved through the snow.

Planting a pole helps you perform any turn. Just as you are shifting onto your downhill edges, plant your downhill pole about one foot (30.5 cm) away from the tip of your ski. Use the pole to mark your turn. Pull it out as you finish the turn.

Be aggressive

When you find yourself moving too fast, doing a **skidded turn** can help control your speed. While performing a skidded turn, put extra pressure on your uphill edges. Your skis will slide and spray out some snow. Add enough pressure to slow down, but not so much that you stop. Bend at your knees and use your lower body to put extra force into your skid. Lean your hips over the inside of the turn. As the turn ends, pull your hips back and straighten your legs a little. Keep your shoulders and hips facing downhill.

Skidded turns are very important to expert skiers on black diamond runs. Doing these turns is the only way to stay in control on steep trails.

Heading to the lifts

The **tuck** is a great stance to use on your way to a lift. This position helps you maintain speed over flat distances, such as at the end of a run. When you notice that the run is about to end, stop turning and ski straight down the fall line. Keep your skis about six inches (15.2 cm) apart, crouch down, and bend your knees. Keep your head up. Place your poles under your arms, pointing backward.

Mogul mania

Once you feel confident turning on smooth slopes, you are ready to try skiing over moguls. A great **mogul field**, or group of moguls, is unpredictable, challenging, and can be a lot of fun. Some moguls are the size of small cars and are very close together, so you'd better be ready! It is best to test your skills on some smaller bumps first.

Turning around the base of a mogul is fairly simple, but it can be slippery. Many skiers turn in these areas, causing patches of ice to form.

Blue bumps

Many blue square runs have small moguls that are widely spaced to give you time to think ahead. You can ski over the bumps or around them. While skiing on moguls, always face downhill. There are two main places to turn on a mogul—around its base and over its **crest**, or top. While turning around the base of a mogul, plant your pole on top of the bump. Then carve or skid around the mogul. To turn on the crest, begin at a slow speed. If you are going too fast, you might launch yourself right off the mogul! Plant your pole on the inside of your turn and let yourself ski down the bump. Bend deeply at the knees as you dig in your uphill edge. As the turn finishes, look ahead to the next mogul.

Turning on the crest of a mogul is exciting. As you improve, you can learn to leave the snow and turn in midair! When you first try this move, use your planted pole as a support.

The ultimate challenge

On smooth runs, you are able to choose when and where you want to turn. In tight mogul fields, however, the bumps choose the turns for you! Big moguls test everything you know about turning. Remember to do your turning movements mainly with your legs. When your shoulders and hips are facing downhill, you have more control and can easily see what is ahead of you.

Up and away

It doesn't take long before skiers want to turn bumps and moguls into their own launching ramps! Landing from jumps is very difficult, however. Do not try jumping off moguls unless you are very comfortable on your skis. While in the air, bend your knees and bring your poles, which are pointing backward, to your sides. Center your weight over your feet and keep your head up. Bend your knees to absorb the impact of the landing.

Before you jump, be sure there are no other skiers in the area where you will land. A crash can cause very serious injuries!

Free at last!

Two popular styles of skiing today are freeskiing and freestyle. These sports are for experts only. Freeskiers explore the **backcountry** to find rough mountain slopes for skiing. They use skis that are designed for quick turns and deep powder. **Bowls** are the favorite spots of freeskiers.

Bowls are giant open areas that are usually on the back side of a mountain. They are often full of deep powder and very steep slopes. Backcountry skiing is exciting, but it is also very dangerous! Skiers who do it must always be careful of **avalanches** and **obstacles**, or objects in the way, such as rocks and trees.

Freeskiing is a great experience for expert skiers. Not only is the terrain challenging, but skiers often get to ski on untouched snow in areas full of powder!

That's tricky!

Freestyle skiers perform tricks that are similar to those done by snowboarders. They even share the same terrain parks. Freestyle tricks include **grab tricks** and **slide tricks**. In a grab trick, skiers hold onto part of their skis while in midair! Slide tricks are done by gliding the skis across metal railings in terrain parks.

*Freestylers use **twin-tip skis**, which are shorter than regular skis and have turned-up tips at both ends. Twin-tips skis are designed to be skied forward or backward and are perfect for performing tricks.*

The right equipment

Terrain parks are playgrounds full of obstacles for freestyle skiers. The halfpipe ramp has two long, steep walls that face each other. Skiers move from one wall to the other and launch themselves up into the air.

*Skiers try to get as much **air**, or height above the ground, as they can to perform grab tricks, **flips**, and **spins**.*

Competitions

Skiing events have been part of the Olympic Winter Games since the 1920s.

A professional downhill racer moves as fast as a car travels on the highway!

Today, there are more types of skiing competitions than ever before. In addition to several styles of racing, there are tournaments for ski jumping, **aerials**, freestyle skiing, and skiing on moguls. Skiing events are very popular at the Olympic Winter Games, where top competitors from all over the world go head-to-head.

I'll race you

There are four main types of alpine skiing races—**slalom**, **giant slalom (GS)**, **super giant slalom (super-G)**, and **downhill**. The courses for slalom, GS, and super-G are marked by **gates**. Skiers have to weave around the gates as they race down the slope. In slalom, the course is fairly short and the gates are close together. In GS, the gates are farther apart and the course is longer. In super-G, skiers race down an even longer course, on which they have never trained before. Downhill racing is just about speed. Racers travel in a tuck position and use their edges as little as possible. They can ski at speeds of over 50 miles per hour (80 kph)! Racers always wear helmets.

It's a bird, it's a plane...

Technical jumping events in skiing have two main styles—ski jumping and aerials. Ski jumpers try to travel the farthest distance. Aerial jumpers attempt to perform creative moves while in midair. Ski jumpers use narrow extra-long ramps to launch themselves into the air. Once airborne, these athletes often travel over 394 feet (120 m) before landing again. That's like jumping over seventeen school buses parked end-to-end! Aerial jumpers do not travel as far, but they do perform dizzying twists and flips before they land. Competitors use a steep ramp to launch themselves straight into the air. Skiers get two chances each to land their jumps. Judges grade their performances on creativity, difficulty, form, and how well the skiers land.

*Ski jumpers do not use poles. Their equipment is designed to be light and **aerodynamic**, or capable of traveling smoothly through the air.*

Anything goes

Terrain-park skiing is not yet an Olympic event, but there are many national and international competitions that allow athletes to show off their amazing talents. Terrain-park skiers attempt to impress judges with creative tricks and giant leaps. The more inventive the skier, the better the result.

Winning the aerials competition requires great concentration and a nearly perfect landing.

Glossary

Note: Boldfaced words that are defined in the text may not appear in the glossary.

aerial A trick performed while the skier is in midair

avalanche A large amount of snow or rock sliding down a mountainside

backcountry A rural area of land where very few people live

biathlon A competition that combines events in cross-country skiing and rifle shooting

competition A contest of ability

cross-country A sport in which skiers travel over the countryside, rather than downhill

cut The design or shape of a ski

fiberglass A material made from glass fibers

flip A trick done by turning head-over-heels while in midair

gate Two poles between which athletes must ski during alpine races

halfpipe A U-shaped ditch with two slopes facing each other

lift attendant A person who checks lift tickets and helps skiers get on the chair lifts safely

ski jumping A competition in which a skier jumps from a ski jump and is judged on both form and the distance jumped

ski patrol Medically trained people who work at a ski resort, attending to injured skiers and enforcing safety rules

spin A turn performed by a skier in the air before landing

stability The state of being balanced and in control of one's movements

terrain An area of land

terrain park A designated area in a ski resort that has ramps and jumps

thermal underwear Undergarments designed to help retain body heat

Index

1 2 3 4 5 6 7 8 9 0   Printed in the U.S.A. 4 3 2 1 0 9 8 7 6 5